Verses From
Northern England

Edited by Claire Tupholme

First published in Great Britain in 2007 by:
Young Writers
Remus House
Coltsfoot Drive
Peterborough
PE2 9JX
Telephone: 01733 890066
Website: www.youngwriters.co.uk

SB ISBN 978-1 84431 122 4

Foreword

Young Writers was established in 1991 and has been passionately devoted to the promotion of reading and writing in children and young adults ever since. The quest continues today. Young Writers remains as committed to the nurturing of poetic and literary talent as ever.

This year's Young Writers competition has proven as vibrant and dynamic as ever and we are delighted to present a showcase of the best poetry from across the UK and in some cases overseas. Each poem has been selected from a wealth of *Little Laureates* entries before ultimately being published in this, our sixteenth primary school poetry series.

Once again, we have been supremely impressed by the overall quality of the entries we have received. The imagination, energy and creativity which has gone into each young writer's entry made choosing the poems a challenging and often difficult but ultimately hugely rewarding task - the general high standard of the work submitted ensured this opportunity to bring their poetry to a larger appreciative audience.

We sincerely hope you are pleased with this final collection and that you will enjoy *Little Laureates Verses From Northern England* for many years to come.

Contents

Hutton Rudby Primary School, Hutton Rudby

Jonathan Webster (7)   28
Isabella Rose-Atkinson & Billy Shaw (7)   29
Robyn Connors (7)   30
Jack Grimston (7)   31
Maximilian Hodgkinson (8)   32
Dominic Bennington (7) & Cameron Twigg (8)   33
Jennifer Stokes (8)   34
Andrew Sawer (8)   35
Erica Brugmans (7) & Anna Fenwick (8)   36
Lucy Shaw (7)   37
James Turnbull (8)   38
Louis Goldsack (7) & James Brooks (8)   39
Georgina Dawson (8)   40
Mina Whiley (7)   41
Emma Devereux (7) & Bethany Robinson (8)   42
Sara Robinson (8)   43
Piers Slade (7)   44
William Parry (7)   45
Angus Forsyth (7)   46
Aran Banerjee (7)   47
Jamie Bennison (8)   48
Tom Honeyman (7)   49
Freddie Wiles (7)   50

Lynnfield CP School, Hartlepool

Rema Uddin   51
Caitlyn Pearce (9)   52
Adriann Strickland (9)   53
Jade Henderson (9)   54
Natasha Stephenson (10)   55
Haleemah Hussain (11)   56
Victoria Sanderson (11)   57
Libby Topping (11)   58
Callum Rayment (10)   59

St Augustine's RC Primary School, Darlington

Christian Brown (9)   60
Rosie Pilling (8)   61
Eleanor Bickle (8)   62
Christian Potter (10)   63

Molly Cunningham (9)	64
Courtney Nicholson (10)	65
Emily Noble (9)	66
Sophie Bainbridge (10)	67
Heather Randle (10)	68
Thomas Smith (11)	69
Dominic Morgan (10)	70
Fern Pearson (10)	71
Katie Noble (11)	72
Pippa McCollom (10)	73
Victoria Lindsay (11)	74
James Gillow (10)	75

St Joseph's RC (VA) Primary School, Newton Aycliffe

Hannah Price (11)	76
Maria O'Hanlon (10)	77
Olivia Gray (10)	78
Rhianne Carson (11)	79
George Lee (10)	80
Anthony Fitzgerald (11)	81
Corey Horn (11)	82
Alicja Szczepanska (10)	83
Emily Mason (10)	84
Steven Bagshaw (9)	85
Anya Harrison (9)	86
Brett Williams (10)	87
Kurtis McKerr (10)	88
James Newton (10)	89
Lewis Clennell (10)	90
Emily Norton (9)	91
Mason Steed (9)	92
Jake Nicholls (9)	93
Joseph Turnbull (9)	94
Rowen Stanier (10)	95
Declan Middleton (9)	96
Ross Garland (9)	97
Sophie Scott (9)	98
Clare Brennan (9)	99
Daniel Smith (9)	100
Elizabeth Driver (10)	101

St Mary's RC Primary School, Consett

Katie Westgarth (10)	102
Jonathan Gorman (9)	103
Daniel James Lister (9)	104
Beth Palmer (9)	105
Abbey Thompson (9)	106
Hope Hilditch (10)	107
Emily Phillips (10)	108
Philip Daly (10)	109
Charlotte Smith (11)	110
Sara Wilson (10)	111
Liam Hicks (10)	112
Eleanor Hill (10)	113
Christopher Ayton (11)	114
Calley Nelson (10)	115
Jesse Foy (11)	116
Kirsty McGray (11)	117
Andrew Lawson (10)	118
Hannah Roberts (10)	119
Charlotte Louise Cousin (10)	120
Rebecca Swinney (10)	121
Alixandra St Julien (10)	122

Wingate Junior School, Wingate

Gabrielle Cameron (10)	123
Adam Leonard	124
Adam Sayle (9)	125
Andrew Nichol (10)	126
Aidan Whiting (8)	127
Connor Holland (10)	128
Rebecca Louise Siddle (11)	129
Bradley Saiger (10)	130
Kimberley Roache (10)	131
Daniel Healer (10)	132
Charlotte Patterson (10)	133
Tony Rowe (9)	134
Hannah Blakelock (11)	135
McKenzie Mason (8)	136
Kieran Baxter (9)	137
Demi Leigh Stanger (9)	138
Dean Wallace (9)	139

The Poems

Death By Pollution

Pollution, pollution, sky pollution,
dull clouds, black clouds and it's as if
it doesn't even exist.
Why can't the sky be like this clear,
gleaming white clouds and a nice blue sky?

The lovely sun is out today shining in our eyes,
bright today, shall it be.
Today is the day the sun goes away, dull and dark,
not a single prick of light to see not today
and not tomorrow and not the next day.

The river is shining, nice and blue
the fish are swimming around the rocks,
Some are blue, some are red and some are orange.
the little fish are dead today, all because of you,
You, you all of us are the ones to blame.
They float around, dead because of this Earth.
All the flowers from around the river are gone, gone, gone
because of you, you, you!

Big and healthy are the trees
they have lived for sixteen years
because of us, they are dead.
No leaves, no twigs and no life in it
all because of us, us, us.

Conor Sullivan (10)
Barnard Grove Primary School, Hartlepool

A Snowy Day

When you're walking in the snow,
you wear a pair of gloves and a hat.
But when you are inside, you get nice and cosy
and sit on a mat.

If you like looking at snow
you should definitely see the sprinkled snow
around the Christmas tree.

Snow is lovely and white,
and if you are far away, it is a great sight.

Snow is brilliant and cold,
and sometimes it looks like shimmering gold.

Arinder Rai (8)
Barnard Grove Primary School, Hartlepool

Death By Pollution

The gleamy sun once shone,
Emerging out to everyone, spotting nothing.
Floating in the sky, dull and misty
Fading away with nothing to see.

The swaying trees, once green,
Cheerful and fresh
Now black, caving in oxygen
No one to notice, mystic and dead.

The sparkling river, streaming calm,
Its shining water not to be seen.
Gleaming in spark
Now an unfed beast.

Unheard and unseen.

Connor Swift (9)
Barnard Grove Primary School, Hartlepool

Pollution

Pollution is dangerous,
It will evolve into a vicious beast,
Tearing our land to shreds,
Biting the Earth.

Pollution will take over,
Will we survive?
Floods and storms will come,
The Earth will tremble.

Pollution reigns,
Its power is too strong,
The world will perish,
Can we stop it?

Pollution is a king,
We are the servants,
It will destroy us,
Our lives are ruined.

Sayhuo Quan (10)
Barnard Grove Primary School, Hartlepool

Peering Through The Grimy Window

Peering through the grimy window, that once was very shiny,
I saw clear blue skies.
Birds soared though the white fluffy clouds
No puffing smoke, but now I see misty blue skies.
Birds scatter and balls of puffy smoke from factories,
Polluting the air.

Peering through the grimy window, that once was very shiny,
I saw clear calm waters.
A home for gentle fish, doing stunts in the bubbles.
Dolphins pouncing in and out of the sea,
But now I see moss floating on top of the black rusty water.
No more fish, no more dolphins.

Peering through the grimy window, that once was very shiny,
I saw tall brown trunks of bark and green emerald leaves shine.
But now I see the bark catching a light and getting taken down
By the huge fire disruption.

Linzi Gardiner (10)
Barnard Grove Primary School, Hartlepool

Pollution

When I look out of the grimy window I look and see
A blue sky with white fluffy clouds
But the way you go on the sky will be grey and dull
With no aeroplanes in sight.
All the clouds will turn coal-black
And soon it will thunder all day long.

When I look out of the grimy window I can see
Shining sapphire rivers
With leaping frogs and scaly fishes.
But soon it will be all russet with a bad smell.
Litter and cans everywhere,
When you look, it will be a dump
With hovering flies all around.

When I look out the grimy window I can see
Some beautiful trees with lots of leaves
Which are emerald-green.
Soon there will be no trees and no leaves anywhere.

Rebecca Popplewell (10)
Barnard Grove Primary School, Hartlepool

Pollution

The bright blue sky that was high before,
Shone with whiteness.
The same bright sky now is dull and low,
Black with mist as if you couldn't see.

The fast shiny river that was clean before
Shone with brightness.
The same bright river that was shiny
Is now dirty with filth.
It's slow and black.

The shiny yellow sun that was bright before
Is high and bright.
The same shiny sun now is mucky and old,
Black with mist.

The tree that was green and colourful
And was leafy before it had a brown trunk,
The same green tree is now muddy with mist and
Is dusty and dull.

Lewis Newbury (10)
Barnard Grove Primary School, Hartlepool

My Family

My family are sweet
It runs in their veins.
My mum helps me with my homework,
Well she's got the brains!

My family are nice,
My family are cool,
My family are fine
And never make me feel like a fool.

Sisters, brothers,
Mums and dads
My family are really not that bad.

Sarah Johnson (10)
Barnard Grove Primary School, Hartlepool

Bonny The Dog

I have a dog called Bonny
She is very funny
When we take her for a walk
She leaps and bounds and tries to talk.

Bethany Austwicke (7)
Barnard Grove Primary School, Hartlepool

Going To School

I am walking to school with a friend,
And I'm very pleased to attend.
School is really, really great,
So try not to be too late.
If you arrive after the bell
All the children will shout and tell.
School starts at fifty minutes past eight,
So at nine o'clock, they lock the school gates.

Chloe Aird (8)
Barnard Grove Primary School, Hartlepool

Water In Our World

Water is clear, glittering and shiny;
the sea is a giant, creased
blanket of silk.
The rain is blue sapphires,
falling from the sky.
The river is a silky scarf looping
around hills.
The waterfall is crystals, falling
towards the ground,
and the lake is a huge
rippled puddle.
Water is clear, glittering and shiny.

Megan Vasey (10)
Coxhoe Primary School, Coxhoe

What Water Can Be

Water can be shimmering rain turned into magnificent seas,
Raindrops are tiny jewels that fall from Heaven.
The river is a slithering slimy snake.
The waterfall is an angel's dress draped over a cliff.
The lake is a pool of blue ice.
The sea is a creased blue blanket, sat over the land.
Water can be shimmering rain turned into magnificent seas.

Jessica McLauchlan
Coxhoe Primary School, Coxhoe

Water Is . . .

Water is clear, glittering, shiny and healthy,
Rain is sparkling diamonds falling from the sky.
The river is pads of blue and white cotton wool.
The waterfall is a creased blanket falling into diamonds.
The lake is a place for everyone to enjoy,
The sea is a blue and white blanket.
Water is clear, glittering, shiny and healthy.

Shona Pell (10)
Coxhoe Primary School, Coxhoe

Water Is Fun For Everyone

Rain is shooting bullets coming from clouds,
The river is winding blue cotton, heading
towards a creased cushion.
The waterfall is a drink trickling down
into my mouth.
The lake is a breath of fresh air
for everyone.
The sea is melted chocolate
looking for space.

Stephen Wadge (10)
Coxhoe Primary School, Coxhoe

My Earth

Tabitha my cat
Purple spiral curtains
Old window sill
Conservatory roof below me
Sheds with my cat Spider sunbathing under the apple tree
Trees swaying
Next-door's screaming is fading away from me
The sea, but not any boats
Cars, tiny dots, zooming away
Surfers riding the sea
Mud at the bottom of the ocean
I could learn to fish.

Bethan Allan (10)
Dormanstown Primary School, Redcar

My Sun

A golden spinning bike wheel
Dazzling on the water
A booming drum full of danger
You have sunspots like the leopard
Melting ice, making water
A precious diamond
You follow me down town.

Lewis Burnett (9)
Dormanstown Primary School, Redcar

I Remember . . .

When I look at the sea
I remember my lost friends
When I look at the rough sea
I remember the bullies at school.

When I look at the seals
I remember when I had fun
When I look at the seagulls
I remember peace.

When I look at the calm waves
I remember my nana
When I look at the starfish on its own
I remember my loneliness.

Ben Kasper (11)
Dormanstown Primary School, Redcar

A Fun Day

I remember as a young boy
I danced in the sun
With a lot of joy.

The sun disappeared
And the wind came out,
I ran to get my kite
While it was still light.

My kite flew and flew
While the wind grew and grew.
Soon I got bored,
So I went indoors.

I went to sit down,
I turned on the TV
And my mam frowned at me.

Conor Miller (11)
Dormanstown Primary School, Redcar

Listen

Can you hear a ladybird creeping
up a tree?

Can you hear a caterpillar sliding
for his tea?

Can you hear a worm sliding
in the mud?

Can you hear a snail crawling
on some wood?

Can you hear a butterfly flapping
his wings?

Can you hear the sand martin as
it gently sings?

Harry Best (8)
Holy Trinity Rosehill CE Primary School, Stockton-on-Tees

Listen

Can you hear a leaf float off a tree?
Can you hear an ant munching on a leaf?
Can you hear a grasshopper jump to and fro?
Can you hear a snail slip and slide?
Can you hear a fox's tail sway in the breeze?
Can you hear a fly swirl round and round?
Can you hear a beetle crawl?
Can you hear a butterfly flutter its wings?

Megan Fisher (8)
Holy Trinity Rosehill CE Primary School, Stockton-on-Tees

Listen

Can you hear a bird flying in the air?
Can you hear a fish swimming in the pond?
Can you hear a cow walking?
Can you hear a duck in the pond?
Can you hear a bee breathe?
Can you hear a shark snapping to eat a fish?

Jacob Jackson
Holy Trinity Rosehill CE Primary School, Stockton-on-Tees

Listen

Can you hear frogs jumping on trees?
Can you hear the sea swirling in and out?
Can you hear a fox swing his tail in the wind?
Can you hear a caterpillar sliding on the ground?

Ellie Bromfield (7)
Holy Trinity Rosehill CE Primary School, Stockton-on-Tees

Look

Can you see huge towers standing still?
Can you see curling towers up against the hill?
Can you see towers in the midnight sky?
Can you see cubes right up high?
Can you see pipes everywhere?
Can you see the stream drifting through the air?
Can you see the sunset rise up on the hill?
Can you see the sunset behind the steelworks
                                    like a giant's Lego?

Jessica Wright (8)
Holy Trinity Rosehill CE Primary School, Stockton-on-Tees

Look

Can you see a tower with vapour coming from the pipes?
Can you see chimneys going up the rusty tank?
Can you see the sand martin flying over the steel tower?
Can you see curving beams floating through the river?
Can you see pylons through a cloudy sky?
Can you see seal sands where seals are?
Can you see bubbling steam lazily rising through the air?
Can you see a pylon?
Can you see criss-crossed sunshine?
Can you see grey hot smoky concrete?

Megan Poppleton (7)
Holy Trinity Rosehill CE Primary School, Stockton-on-Tees

Listen!

Can you hear a fox tiptoeing across the ground?
Can you hear a frog jumping into a tree?
Can you hear the sea swaying from side to side?
Can you hear a bird flying in the sky?
Can you hear a butterfly crunching on some leaves?

Lily Rose Macaulay (7)
Holy Trinity Rosehill CE Primary School, Stockton-on-Tees

The Magic Box

(Based on 'Magic Box' by Kit Wright)

I will put in my box . . .
The cold breeze of a winter's night,
A drop of the finest water from over the world
And the colours of a butterfly.

I will put inside my box . . .
The best strip of wood ever seen,
A giant with a rumbling belly
And the roar of a loan.

I will put inside my box . . .
A flash of lightning and a golden sun.
Islands and promontories
And a silver sea.

My box is fashioned from diamonds
From the darkest caves
With secrets from our Lord
And the toe joints of a tiger.

I shall sleep with my box on the finest bed ever made,
Then ride to the beach,
The colour of the sun.

Matthew Harry Wilson (8)
Holy Trinity Rosehill CE Primary School, Stockton-on-Tees

The Magic Box

(Based on 'Magic Box' by Kit Wright)

I will put in my magic Teesside box . . .
The sound of the seagulls squawking,
The sight of the dark sea swishing and
The feeling of a soft seal's back.

I will put in my magic Teesside box . . .
All the noises of steam, gushing out of tubes
And the peace of lakes sleeping in the marsh.

I will put in my magic Teesside box . . .
The leaping of seven seals in the sea and
The soft spongy green moss stuck
In the middle of the pavement.

I will put in my magic Teesside box . . .
Green buds ready to burst and the
Cream and brown reeds swaying in the wind.

My magic Teesside box is green
With sapphire jewels and patterned with
Swirls in gold.

I will put in my magic Teesside box . . .
All the memories of my trip to Seal Sands.

Katie Cain (8)
Holy Trinity Rosehill CE Primary School, Stockton-on-Tees

The Christmas Tree

One red and white angel guarding the tree.
Two wondrous baubles, glistening with white.
Three marching soldiers, one red, one white, one green.
Four loud instruments being played like mad.
Five shining stars, big and small.
Six red baubles glowing in the dark,
Seven little presents on golden strings.
Eight packets of chocolate, which are so yummy to eat.
Nine little bells, tinkling away,
Ten Christmas crackers going off with a boom
And there, at the bottom of our Christmas tree
Are two big presents, waiting for me!

Jonathan Webster (7)
Hutton Rudby Primary School, Hutton Rudby

Robberphobia

I am scared of robbers
Like a tyre terrified of a nail
Like winter is petrified of spring
Like a pen is of paper
Like an apple is frightened of a worm
Like a tree horrified of an axe
I am scared of a robber.

Isabella Rose-Atkinson & Billy Shaw (7)
Hutton Rudby Primary School, Hutton Rudby

Small Sally

There's a monster in the loft
With eyes as big as balls
It lives in a corner
Where my mum keeps her shawls.

My mum calls it Sally, she says
She creeps each day
Into people's bedrooms
(When my horse goes neigh!)

I lie and hear her coming
Creeping down the stairs
I look quickly behind but there's nobody there!

Robyn Connors (7)
Hutton Rudby Primary School, Hutton Rudby

Shark Phobia

I am scared of sharks
Like an apple is horrified of a mouth
Like a tyre is terrified of a nail
Like a football is frightened of a foot
Like autumn is afraid of winter
Like a pen is afraid of paper
I am scared of sharks.

Jack Grimston (7)
Hutton Rudby Primary School, Hutton Rudby

Autumn Has Returned

It's autumn and the garden is changing its clothes
putting away its blue sleeveless top
its dotty green swimming shorts
and orange sandals.

Now it wraps itself in spiky conker shell gloves,
a twirled black tree jumper
and thick orange trousers.

Maximilian Hodgkinson (8)
Hutton Rudby Primary School, Hutton Rudby

Arachnophobia

I am scared of spiders
Like paper is nervous of scissors
Like a rocket is afraid of a black hole
Like chocolate is petrified of teeth
Like the Black Pearl is horrified of the Kraken
Like a ruler is frightened of Joseph
I am scared of spiders.

Dominic Bennington (7) & Cameron Twigg (8)
Hutton Rudby Primary School, Hutton Rudby

A Poem To Be Spoken Silently

(Based on 'A Poem to be Spoken Silently' by Pie Corbett)

It was so quiet that I heard
the wind blowing my hair about.

It was so quiet that I heard
a butterfly spread its beautiful wings gently.

It was so quiet that I heard
a golden leaf float in the air.

It was so quiet that I heard
a worm slither in the mud

It was so quiet that I heard
the clouds drift across the sky.

Jennifer Stokes (8)
Hutton Rudby Primary School, Hutton Rudby

A Poem To Be Spoken Silently

(Based on 'A Poem to be Spoken Silently' by Pie Corbett)

It was so quiet that I heard
A robin's wings delicately flapping.

It was so quiet that I heard
A conker split open and drop to the ground.

It was so quiet that I heard
A goldfish gliding across the pond.

It was so quiet that I heard
Smoke drifting up in the air.

It was so quiet that I heard
A hedgehog snuffling along.

Andrew Sawer (8)
Hutton Rudby Primary School, Hutton Rudby

Petrifying Penny

There's a devil in the garden
With horns as big as knives
It lives in the sandpit
Where my grandad keeps the flies.

My brother calls it Penny
He says she creeps each morning
Into people's gardens
(When night stops falling).

I sit and feel her coming
I hear her silent feet
I hide behind the bed
And she'll turn me into meat.

Erica Brugmans (7) & Anna Fenwick (8)
Hutton Rudby Primary School, Hutton Rudby

A Poem To Be Spoken Silently

(Based on 'A Poem to be Spoken Silently' by Pie Corbett)

It was so quiet that I heard
a fly wrap its greedy hands together.

It was so quiet that I heard
toys open up under the Earth.

It was so quiet that I heard
a butterfly flapping its wings.

Lucy Shaw (7)
Hutton Rudby Primary School, Hutton Rudby

A Poem To Be Spoken Silently

(Based on 'A Poem to be Spoken Silently' by Pie Corbett)

It was so quiet that I heard a bird's wing
flap into the distance.

It was so quiet that I heard a worm move
its slimy body through the soil.

It was so quiet that I heard a ladybird
crawl along a spike of grass.

It was so quiet that I heard the sunset
in the evening sky.

It was so quiet that I heard the stars
light up in the black night.

James Turnbull (8)
Hutton Rudby Primary School, Hutton Rudby

The Munching Monster

There's a monster in the attic
With a snout as wet as rain
It lives in a wardrobe
And it has a gigantic cane.

My brother calls it 'The Munching Monster'
He says it creeps each fortnight
Into my bedroom
(When I play with my kite).

Louis Goldsack (7) & James Brooks (8)
Hutton Rudby Primary School, Hutton Rudby

The Christmas Tree

One golden twinkly angel with a long white dress
Two sparkly pine cones making a mess
Three glimmering fairies shining in the light
Four blue baubles shimmering in yellow brightness
Five brown robins waiting to chirp
Six white snowflakes glistening like snow
Seven flittering snow-girls on glittery strings
Eight pink ribbons hanging off the tree
Nine shining fairies making a colourful room
Ten stripy candy sticks waiting to be eaten
And there at the bottom of my Christmas tree
Is a lumpy red stocking, waiting for me!

Georgina Dawson (8)
Hutton Rudby Primary School, Hutton Rudby

It's Autumn

A half-eaten leaf blowing
In the raging wind,
The smell of wood in the air.
An acorn swaying in the wind,
A feather has fallen.
The signs of autumn.

Mina Whiley (7)
Hutton Rudby Primary School, Hutton Rudby

Huge Harry

There's a ghost in the attic
With eyes as big as clocks
It lives in a box
Where my dad keeps the blocks.

My brother calls it Harry
He says it creeps each dark day
Into children's bedrooms
Where my friends used to stay.

Emma Devereux (7) & Bethany Robinson (8)
Hutton Rudby Primary School, Hutton Rudby

Autumn Is Here

It's autumn
And the garden is changing its clothes,
Putting away
Its pink and red flip-flops
With raspberries all over.
Its purple top with a picture of blossom on.

It's getting out its brown crinkly-leaved coat
with acorn buttons,
Blue trousers with all sorts of berries on.
White boots with red leaves and gooseberries on.
Autumn is here.

Sara Robinson (8)
Hutton Rudby Primary School, Hutton Rudby

Autumn Has Returned

It's autumn
And the garden is changing its clothes,
Putting away
Its light blue flowery swimming shorts.
Its perfect red short-sleeved tops
And rotten green-grass shorts.

Now it wraps itself in brown, dull
Tree-coloured scarves.
A conkershell woolly hat.
It is now relaxing in the breezing wind.
Autumn has returned.

Piers Slade (7)
Hutton Rudby Primary School, Hutton Rudby

Autumn Has Returned

It's autumn
The garden is changing its clothes
She is putting away
Her green leafy tops
Her brown twisted shorts
And her red apple socks

Now she wraps herself in a crunchy leaf coat
An acorn sweatshirt to keep warm
Some thick plum trousers
Now she rests in a deep pile of compost
Autumn has returned.

William Parry (7)
Hutton Rudby Primary School, Hutton Rudby

It's Autumn

It's autumn
and the garden's face is shining
like one hundred lights in your room,
The garden's arms are like lizards
wiggling as fast as they can.

The garden has flowers on his jeans and
the animals are hibernating.
The garden is changing his clothes in autumn and
Autumn is here.

Angus Forsyth (7)
Hutton Rudby Primary School, Hutton Rudby

Autumn Is Here

It's autumn,
The garden is changing her clothes,
She is putting away her
Sunflower T-shirt
And her white petalled shorts.

Now she puts on her twig-white hat,
Her leafy gold coat.
Her brown, wilting plant jeans,
And her dark bare tree boots.
Then she rests in the breezy wind,
Autumn is here.

Aran Banerjee (7)
Hutton Rudby Primary School, Hutton Rudby

A Poem To Be Spoken Silently

(Based on 'A Poem to be Spoken Silently' by Pie Corbett)

It was so quiet that I heard a cloud split into rain,
It was so quiet that I heard a butterfly spread its beautiful wings.
It was so quiet that I heard a leaf sway down to the soil.
It was so quiet that I heard some yellow paint dry in the breeze.
It was so quiet that I heard my heart beat.

Jamie Bennison (8)
Hutton Rudby Primary School, Hutton Rudby

A Poem To Be Spoken Silently

(Based on 'A Poem to be Spoken Silently' by Pie Corbett)

It was so quiet that I heard a plant die.
It was so quiet that I heard some ants wriggle along the sofa.
It was so quiet that I heard a butterfly flap its wings.
It was so quiet that I heard a worm slither along the soil.
It was so quiet that I heard a bird swoop to the ground.

Tom Honeyman (7)
Hutton Rudby Primary School, Hutton Rudby

A Poem To Be Spoken Silently

(Based on 'A Poem to be Spoken Silently' by Pie Corbett)

It was so quiet that I heard a golden leaf slowly drift to the ground.
It was so quiet that I heard a worm crack through the soft
summer earth.
It was so quiet that I heard a bird soar across the sky.
It was so quiet that I heard a tiny hair sprout
out of my skin.
It was so quiet that I heard a new conker slowly grow.

Freddie Wiles (7)
Hutton Rudby Primary School, Hutton Rudby

Snow Is Coming

Snow is coming, get ready to play
Dance, dance every day.
Snow is soft, snow is fluffy,
Snow is cold, snow is icy.

Snow is coming, get ready to fight,
Throw balls with all your might.
Snow is there to slip along,
Now you know where you belong.

Rema Uddin
Lynnfield CP School, Hartlepool

Shooting Star

Whoosh!
A shot of red
A glance of glitter
It's a shooting star
All cold and bitter.

As fast as a rocket
As small as a locket.

So yellow and shiny
Too tiny
To hold.

Caitlyn Pearce (9)
Lynnfield CP School, Hartlepool

Heaven

H is for Heaven that is above us
E is for everyone because everyone goes there
A is for anyone because anyone can go there
V is for valuable which Heaven is
E is for excited, which we get
N is for never, because Heaven never ends.

Adriann Strickland (9)
Lynnfield CP School, Hartlepool

My Little Sister

My little sister is a twister
She's on the run
While she's full of fun
That's my little sister.

My little sister
She's a waster
While she's a taster
For Mum's cake
That's my little sister.

My little sister
Is full of joy
She's always playing with her toy
What a shame she wasn't a boy
That's my little sister.

Jade Henderson (9)
Lynnfield CP School, Hartlepool

Help, Help My Sister Is On Fire!

Help, help my sister is set on fire,
She's running round like a cheetah,
Roaring like a lion,
Jumping like a leopard,
Quacking like a duck,
Flapping like a chicken
And waddling like a penguin.
It's like she's in a zoo.
Just help, help before
She wakes Mum and Dad!

Natasha Stephenson (10)
Lynnfield CP School, Hartlepool

My Nephew

My nephew is a star,
he really likes cars,
I love him a lot
and he sleeps in a cot.

He always winds me up
and drinks water in a cup.
He pulls his socks up high
and he always waves me goodbye.

My nephew is simply the best,
but at times can be a pest,
He loves going to the town,
and has a thing for clowns.

He likes writing with a pen
and loves his friend Ben,
He likes the soft white snow,
but only because it makes his face glow.

He likes playing football
and always has a nasty fall,
He lives in Hartlepool
and he is really very cool.

Haleemah Hussain (11)
Lynnfield CP School, Hartlepool

Every Night I Dance

Dance, dance, dance, dance up the stairs
For all hours on end
I do lots and lots of tricks
Do the splits and skip
This is what I do every night!

Victoria Sanderson (11)
Lynnfield CP School, Hartlepool

My Friends

I believe in angels
the sort that Heaven sends
I'm surrounded by angels
but I call them my friends.

Libby Topping (11)
Lynnfield CP School, Hartlepool

My Dream

My dream is quite unusual, not many people see
That one day a pro-dancer I'd really like to be.
This dance that I like doing is ballroom and Latin style
It makes me feel good inside, so much that I only want to smile.
So one day in years to come and you pass me by and catch
a glance.
Just remember when you knew me, all I wanted to do
Is dance.

Some days, it's very hard and really quite upsetting
Because some people don't understand all the fun that I'm getting.
Calling me names and saying nasty things, doesn't really bother me,
Because one day I will be a winner and then you all will see.

My heroes are not footballers or singers, I dare not even tell,
My hero is a brilliant dancer, by the name of Adele.

Callum Rayment (10)
Lynnfield CP School, Hartlepool

The Glistening Moon

The moon glows
Like a pot of silver
In a spotty coat
Which is held by the stars
The clouds fly past
Watching the moon glisten
In the night sky.

Christian Brown (9)
St Augustine's RC Primary School, Darlington

Winter Nights' Moon

Moon rises, sun falls, night comes,
Darkness swallows up the light.
The moon is like a white snowball in the sky,
The moon shines on winter nights.

Rosie Pilling (8)
St Augustine's RC Primary School, Darlington

The Moon Shines

The moon is like a pebble in the sky,
When I look out of the window, I see a glimmering face
looking at me.
When I look at the moon, it seems like a white marble
in the sky.

The moon is like a giant football in the sky,
The moon reminds me of another world in space,
It seems to me like a rocky mountain.

The moon to me is like a white round biscuit,
The moon seems to me like a white round firework,
The moon is like a white round TV in the sky.

Eleanor Bickle (8)
St Augustine's RC Primary School, Darlington

Dark Night

On a dark night
When the fireflies are alight
Long faces pale and thin as laces
Vanishing into the dark sky

In kennels, barns and fields
And down in the burrows
Where animals sleep
There's not a sound, not a peep

The whisper of darkness
Cannot be heard
As it wraps around
The sound of a word.

Christian Potter (10)
St Augustine's RC Primary School, Darlington

My Idol

My grandma is my idol,
She is very kind, never mean
And whenever I'm upset
She's always there, listening to me.

My grandma is my idol,
She makes terrific macaroni cheese,
But when I ask for seconds, she says, 'No!'
And I always say, 'Oh please!'

My grandma is my idol,
She's kind and caring too.
I only see her rarely though
But I'm going to see her tomorrow so
Woo hoo!

Molly Cunningham (9)
St Augustine's RC Primary School, Darlington

My Pet Cat

When I see my pet cat
I really, really feel so happy.
Every time I get home
My cat looks a bit fatter.

When I get up in the morning,
She makes me feel warm.
When I leave my school uniform downstairs,
I find her snuggled up on top.

When my cat was a kitten
That was when I brought her home.
When I feed her fish
She cleans out the entire dish.

When my cat is older,
I will be really sorry,
So I wish cats really
Had nine lives.

Courtney Nicholson (10)
St Augustine's RC Primary School, Darlington

What If?

What if trees were yellow
And birds couldn't sing
And if flowers were dull
And bells didn't ring?

What if houses were always small
And bees couldn't buzz
And people were too tall
And what if rabbits didn't hop?

What if we had orange and yellow stars
And cats didn't climb trees?
What if we lived on Mars?
Oh, what would we do?

Emily Noble (9)
St Augustine's RC Primary School, Darlington

My Best Friend

My best friend keeps secrets,
She doesn't say a word
And nobody knows her name.
She makes me giggle a lot.

My best friend is my only friend,
Nobody can see her, she is never around,
The only thing I don't like about her
Is that I made her up in my mind.

Sophie Bainbridge (10)
St Augustine's RC Primary School, Darlington

My Neighbour's Cat

My neighbour's cat is called Smudge
She is really big and fluffy
I like to stroke her bushy tail
As she scratches her back against the tree.

My neighbour's cat is brown and white
And her coat is shiny and glossy
She has these cute big golden eyes
And she looks so innocent (although she isn't).

Heather Randle (10)
St Augustine's RC Primary School, Darlington

Evil Cloud

The evil cloud, the evil cloud
Drifting high above the ground,
You can hear the thunder rumbling loud
Look, there's another evil cloud I've found.

There in the sky, a groaning face,
No, no that's the cloud, the evil one.
It's starting to frighten me!
Yeah me too, but look it's going to strike.

It's polluting the whole town
Some people are getting ill.
Argh! Someone has died,
This whole town is contaminated.

Thomas Smith (11)
St Augustine's RC Primary School, Darlington

War!

The swish of a sword,
The stretch of the bowstring.
The army trembling on their feet
As they get ready for war.

The opponents are seen up on a hill,
The bowmen getting ready,
The opponents are getting closer,
'Fire!' shouts the king.

Most of the arrows miss but a few hit.
It's the end of the war and soldiers are going home.
Relieved families, crying with joy,
So the end of the war.
I hope there is no more war.

Dominic Morgan (10)
St Augustine's RC Primary School, Darlington

My Dream

My dream is to be a star
Wandering high and low
To watch the world go by
People walk to and fro

My dream is to be a star
Twinkling bright
All the night
Even when it's not bright.

Fern Pearson (10)
St Augustine's RC Primary School, Darlington

The Land Of Sweets

The Land Of Sweets is my favourite place to be,
There's lots to do and lots to see.
You can try the sweets, tasting of raspberries and strawberries,
It's up to you what you want to do.

Come with me and I'll take you there,
But don't tell anyone, oh no, don't you dare!
Or you'll have to answer to me, so beware.
Come with me, I'll take you there.

Katie Noble (11)
St Augustine's RC Primary School, Darlington

Ghost Girl

Everybody ignores her
Nobody is her friend,
Everyone acts like she's invisible,
Nobody notices her.

She walks through the corridors,
All lonely, all cold.
Everybody is chatting,
She feels so excluded.

The clock strikes midnight,
She feels so alone.
She feels so alone,
She just can't take it anymore.

She looks at the window,
She looks out of the window.
She opens it,
She jumps.

A shriek
A scream!
Is it a dream?
No, she's dead!

Nobody knows her name,
Nobody is her friend.
Nobody will notice she is dead
For nobody is her friend.

Pippa McCollom (10)
St Augustine's RC Primary School, Darlington

Pets

I have a parrot named Charlie,
He is a very happy chap,
He flies round in his cage all day
But sometimes takes a nap.

I have a bunny named Molly,
She is a very active girl.
She runs around in the garden
But likes to nibble on a Twirl.

I have a dog named Rover,
He's a very lazy lad.
He always chews my clothes up
My mum says he's very bad.

I have a very smelly house
Because it's like a zoo.
There are animals running everywhere,
But there's always fighting too.

Victoria Lindsay (11)
St Augustine's RC Primary School, Darlington

The Potato Of Doom

P hilistine warrior, ready to attack,
O ver the hills, that's where they're at.
T urnip Troopers, waiting for us
A ngry as a teenage boy, ready to fight,
T omatoes come in leagues over the seas,
O nly what we want is a pile of peas.

James Gillow (10)
St Augustine's RC Primary School, Darlington

A Limerick

There once was a man called Bill Dick,
Who was literally as thick as a stick.
One day he went to school
And found that he was not really cool.
Now his best friend is Thick Mick.

Hannah Price (11)
St Joseph's RC (VA) Primary School, Newton Aycliffe

A Limerick

The teacher went out to play
But Miss Angry wasn't in that day.
The students all cried
The children survived
And everyone got their own way.

Maria O'Hanlon (10)
St Joseph's RC (VA) Primary School, Newton Aycliffe

A Limerick

There once was a lady from Crewe
Off to Spain she flew
She met her friend called Jake
Who made her a cake
And then she caught the flu.

Olivia Gray (10)
St Joseph's RC (VA) Primary School, Newton Aycliffe

A Limerick

I know a little girl called Kay
Who was born on a very strange day
She was a little fat
And had a black cat
But her birthday was actually in May.

Rhianne Carson (11)
St Joseph's RC (VA) Primary School, Newton Aycliffe

A Limerick

There was a woman called Ms Clauble
Who had one favourite bauble
While holding her cup
The bauble blew up
And all she could do was dawdle.

George Lee (10)
St Joseph's RC (VA) Primary School, Newton Aycliffe

A Limerick

There was a man called Fred
Who didn't like to go to bed
And one day he stayed up late
And *forgot* about his big date
Meanwhile his big date said, 'He's dead.'

Anthony Fitzgerald (11)
St Joseph's RC (VA) Primary School, Newton Aycliffe

A Limerick

There was a Boro fan,
Who drove in a red van
One day he broke down
With a horrible frown
And got out and ran!

Corey Horn (11)
St Joseph's RC (VA) Primary School, Newton Aycliffe

A Limerick

There was a young man called Jake
Who made a cake,
He did it at night
As he wasn't very bright
And he knew it was a very big mistake.

Alicja Szczepanska (10)
St Joseph's RC (VA) Primary School, Newton Aycliffe

A Limerick

There was a young girl from Spain,
Who liked to sing in the rain.
She said, 'I need a fella.'
And bought an umbrella
And never sang in the rain again!

Emily Mason (10)
St Joseph's RC (VA) Primary School, Newton Aycliffe

Anger

Anger is black and scary,
It smells like burning fire.
It sounds like bombs blowing up inside your body.
Anger lives in a deep, dark place, somewhere in your heart.

Steven Bagshaw (9)
S Joseph's RC (VA) Primary School, Newton Aycliffe

Care

Care is baby blue,
Soft and cuddly, just like you.
It smells like a rose in a meadow,
And tastes like dark melting chocolate.
It is the sound of gentle music floating in the air.
It lives in the pot of gold at the end of the rainbow.

Anya Harrison (9)
St Joseph's RC (VA) Primary School, Newton Aycliffe

Anger

Anger is pure black.
It smells like burning wood.
It tastes like bitter milk.
It sounds like a screeching chalk.
It feels sharp and rough.
Anger lives in a dark cave.

Brett Williams (10)
St Joseph's RC (VA) Primary School, Newton Aycliffe

War

War is black and red.
It smells of smoky air.
It tastes sour.
It sounds like loud noises in the air.
It feels sharp and spiky.
It lives on the battlefield.

Kurtis McKerr (10)
St Joseph's RC (VA) Primary School, Newton Aycliffe

War

War is like a jet-black night,
It smells like a dead carcass.
It tastes like blood running through your teeth.
It sounds like cannons booming and rifles firing.
War feels cold and wet, gloopy and gloomy.
It lives in no-man's-land where rats live.

James Newton (10)
St Joseph's RC (VA) Primary School, Newton Aycliffe

War

War is horrible dark brown.
It smells like manure.
War tastes of sour milk.
It sounds like the banging of drums.
It feels hurtful.
War lives in a muddy terrain.

Lewis Clennell (10)
St Joseph's RC (VA) Primary School, Newton Aycliffe

Love

Love is bright sunshine-yellow.
It smells like flowers in full bloom.
It's like burning candles on a fireplace in the middle of winter,
Giving a warm, soft glow.
Love sounds like soft, peaceful music.
It feels like a soft silky quilt.

Emily Norton (9)
St Joseph's RC (VA) Primary School, Newton Aycliffe

Peace

Peace is light pink,
Peace smells like minty ice cream melting in your mouth,
It sounds like a butterfly flying up and up,
Peace tastes like a big plop of rain falling from the sky,
It feels like a big cushion,
Peace lives in a big balloon floating around and around.

Mason Steed (9)
St Joseph's RC (VA) Primary School, Newton Aycliffe

Love

Love is dark red.
It feels like the fast beating of your heart.
It smells like hot chocolate on a cold day.
It tastes like delicious vanilla ice cream.
It sounds like a peaceful tune.
It's all around.

Jake Nicholls (9)
St Joseph's RC (VA) Primary School, Newton Aycliffe

Love

Love is pure gold.
It smells like mountain air.
It tastes divine, like hot chocolate fudge cake.
Love sounds like a harp being strummed by an angel.
It feels soft and warm like a duvet.
Love lives in Heaven.

Joseph Turnbull (9)
St Joseph's RC (VA) Primary School, Newton Aycliffe

Excitement

Excitement is red, yellow, orange, green, purple, pink and blue
Just like the rainbow.
Excitement tastes sugary pink like candyfloss on your tongue.
Excitement smells like the hot dog stand at a funfair.
It sounds like a cheering crowd, jumping up and down, clapping.
It feels like a big yellow sponge being squeezed tightly.
It lives in your stomach with the flying butterflies.

Rowen Stanier (10)
St Joseph's RC (VA) Primary School, Newton Aycliffe

Joy

Joy is bright blue.
It tastes like sugar melting on your tongue.
It sounds like ringing bells and children's laughter.
It feels like a ring of happiness.
It is as gentle as a warm breeze.
It lives in the middle of your heart.

Declan Middleton (9)
St Joseph's RC (VA) Primary School, Newton Aycliffe

Joy

Joy is yellow.
It smells like fresh cut flowers.
It tastes of chocolate buttons.
It sounds like laughing children
And feels like a soft warm blanket.
It lives in Heaven.

Ross Garland (9)
St Joseph's RC (VA) Primary School, Newton Aycliffe

Love

Love is a deep red,
It smells like sweet roses.
It tastes like warm hot chocolate.
Love feels soft and warm.
It sounds like sweet music and lives in us.

Sophie Scott (9)
St Joseph's RC (VA) Primary School, Newton Aycliffe

Love

Love is the colour of soft gentle pinks, oranges and reds.
It tastes like chewy sugary sweets melting in your mouth.
Love smells like fresh air on a hot warm day
And feels like a smooth soft pillow at night.
Love sounds like two chirping baby birds high up in their nest.
It lives deep in the heart of a warm cosy cottage.

Clare Brennan (9)
St Joseph's RC (VA) Primary School, Newton Aycliffe

Happiness

Happiness is bright yellow.
It smells like a field of daisies.
It tastes like ice cream in the summer.
It sounds like birds chirping in a tree in spring.
It feels like a warm fuzzy bear.
Happiness lives deep in your heart.

Daniel Smith (9)
St Joseph's RC (VA) Primary School, Newton Aycliffe

Panic

Panic is blue and grey,
It smells like smoke,
It tastes like salty pizza,
Panic sounds like a high-pitched scream,
It feels like a rough rock,
Panic lives underground in mines.

Elizabeth Driver (10)
St Joseph's RC (VA) Primary School, Newton Aycliffe

My Journey

My life begins at my birth,
The first time I came to Earth,
I came to find
A family I'd always had in mind.

A mam to love
It is like she was sent from above,
A dad who is best,
Ten times better than all the rest!

Two brothers like creatures
Who could never be teachers,
Grandparents with care
And nice white hair!

I started school at the age of four
Who knew it would have been such a *bore,*
My friends at school
Are the only thing that's cool.

Then I came to the junior end
Where some of the teachers drive me round the bend,
A holiday came, time for fun,
We get to play in the sun.

I came to the top of the school,
One more year wouldn't that be cool,
Preparation for our SATs test,
They want to have the score that is the best.

So now I've told about my life,
Filled with love and no need for strife,
With memories that are the best by far,
I will write again when I get a car.

Katie Westgarth (10)
St Mary's RC Primary School, Consett

Love

Love, love, love
Love is dependent, it never lies.
Love is ugly and lovely!
Love is unique in every way.
Love is giving and forgiving!
Love is love.

Jonathan Gorman (9)
St Mary's RC Primary School, Consett

Love

Love is faithful and kind
Love is the heart and soul
Love is a gift of happiness
Love is free and kind
Love is honest and the truth of life
Love is everything and everywhere
Love is next to you night and day.

Daniel James Lister (9)
St Mary's RC Primary School, Consett

Love

L ove can last forever
O r can fade away whenever
V icious as it comes you then have to pay the price
E ven though it's sometimes flirty and nice.

Beth Palmer (9)
St Mary's RC Primary School, Consett

Love!

Love is friendly,
Love is honest,
Love is free.
Love is what you want it to be,
Love leads you to ups and downs.
Love is the most valuable thing a person could ever have.

Abbey Thompson (9)
St Mary's RC Primary School, Consett

Love Is . . .

Dedicated to my dog Riley
Love is happy when with your love,
Love is sad when you've lost it,
Love is like puppy love just jumping out for you,
You miss it when it's gone,
It feels like your world's fallen apart.
Love can be jealous with anger and hate.
Love is what you want it to be!

Hope Hilditch (10)
St Mary's RC Primary School, Consett

Ultimate Love

Love is like . . .
Floods of laughter,
Seas of sorrow,
Unique to you
And a friend to everyone.
But to the heart
It's much, much more.

Emily Phillips (10)
St Mary's RC Primary School, Consett

Love Is . . .

Love is like a magical wall around your heart.
It is wonderful, important and very amazing.
But love is a truthful, honest friend to you
And that's what love is.

Philip Daly (10)
St Mary's RC Primary School, Consett

Love Is . . .

Love is kind, not selfish, not bad,
Love is happy, joyful and glad,
Love is peaceful,
Loyal not proud,
Love is important,
Perfect and never gives up.

Charlotte Smith (11)
St Mary's RC Primary School, Consett

My Love Poem

Love is not selfish,
It is caring.
Love is not ill-mannered,
It is priceless.
Love is not evil,
It is passionate.
Love is the most irresistibly
Burning thing in the world.

Sara Wilson (10)
St Mary's RC Primary School, Consett

Love Is . . .

L ove is priceless
O utgoing love is
V ery red as a red bed, love is
E verlasting and unavoidable, love is not

I rritating but peaceful, love is not
S adly upsetting but is all about happiness.

Liam Hicks (10)
St Mary's RC Primary School, Consett

Love Is . . .

L ove is kind and happy,
O utstanding and loyal,
V ery pure is love,
E veryone feels love,

I t comes from your heart,
S elfish is not what love is.

Eleanor Hill (10)
St Mary's RC Primary School, Consett

Love Is . . .

L iking and kind
O verwhelming and priceless
V ery hot and burning
E very moment of every day love has inside

I nside love is cosy and warm
S ome love is never-ending.

Christopher Ayton (11)
St Mary's RC Primary School, Consett

Love Is . . .

Like a flower so delicate,
It needs someone to keep it warm and care for it
And it needs loyalty
For as long as we all forever live.

Calley Nelson (10)
St Mary's RC Primary School, Consett

Love Is . . .

Love is always round me,
Its warm glow surrounds us all
And it will never ever leave.
If you look around you,
You will see it everywhere.
Love is the feeling of the heart,
The only feeling that God made Himself.

Jesse Foy (11)
St Mary's RC Primary School, Consett

Love Is . . .

Peaceful and never-ending and it never gives up.
Love is hope for everyone I see and it is pure.
Love is red, the colour of appreciation of love.
Love also is pride for your family.
If my family love me your family will love you!

Kirsty McGray (11)
St Mary's RC Primary School, Consett

Love Is . . .

You are kind and priceless,
You are truthful and without hate,
You are the unforgettable,
You are *love!*

You are the thump in a heart,
You are the never-ending,
You are the greater than great,
You are the indescribable.

Andrew Lawson (10)
St Mary's RC Primary School, Consett

Cheesy Feet!

Cheesy feet are smellier than meat
Cheesy feet are not at all sweet
Cheesy feet are much worse in the heat
Cheesy feet are best under the seat.

Hannah Roberts (10)
St Mary's RC Primary School, Consett

My Hamster Chester

My hamster Chester sleeps all day,
He comes out at night
Because he loves to play.
He runs on his wheel round and round,
Oh how he makes a rackety sound.
He runs up his tubes storing food,
If you disturb him he'll go in a mood.
He looks like a bear when he stands on hind legs,
But his feet are just small like tiny little pegs.

Charlotte Louise Cousin (10)
St Mary's RC Primary School, Consett

The Whale

The biggest mammal of them all,
The freedom of the seas,
As big as two double-decker buses,
As gentle as a lamb,
Soon to be extinct,
We hope it won't be.

Rebecca Swinney (10)
St Mary's RC Primary School, Consett

Love Is . . .

L ove is my life
O ut of this world for me
V ery kind in my likings
E verybody is being loved.

I t is in my heart forever.
S aying thanks for my love.

Alixandra St Julien (10)
St Mary's RC Primary School, Consett

Flowers

F lowers are colourful
L ike sunset in the evening
O range and purple
W allflower on the wall
E veryone loves the amazing colours
R ed and orange, yellow too.

Gabrielle Cameron (10)
Wingate Junior School, Wingate

Water

Water can be hot
Just like fire
I wouldn't like to be in it
It's just not my desire

Water can be slow
Water can be fast
If I run it forever
Will it last?

Adam Leonard
Wingate Junior School, Wingate

Flowers

F lowers are colourful.
L ots of flowers are better.
O ther flowers smell better.
W here are the flowers?
E very flower is different.
R ed, yellow, blue are colours of flowers.
S pring is when they bloom.

Adam Sayle (9)
Wingate Junior School, Wingate

Chocolate

Chocolate is runny
Only when it's sunny

When it's runny
It trickles down my throat like honey
At Easter we eat it in the form of a bunny

Buying the lovely bunny is good money
Looking at it is ever so funny.

Andrew Nichol (10)
Wingate Junior School, Wingate

Springtime

S pring is good I like it
P lay in the garden
R abbits have their babies
 I n spring there are fun times
N ow the lambs are born
G ardens are colourful.

Aidan Whiting (8)
Wingate Junior School, Wingate

My Brother

My brother is nice
He eats all the rice
He's scared of mice

He eats all day
He plays with clay
He likes sitting on the beach
He likes sitting on the bay
Only joking, there's no way.

Connor Holland (10)
Wingate Junior School, Wingate

Poppy

Poppy is a tremendous cat
She roams about the street
She turns her head around and around
She never ends on her feet

Poppy, Poppy, oh Poppy
Why do you get so down?
Don't be glum
Just turn around.

Rebecca Louise Siddle (11)
Wingate Junior School, Wingate

My Family

My family are the best.
They are better than the rest.
Mum and Dad they are alright,
But they always get into a fight.

Bradley Saiger (10)
Wingate Junior School, Wingate

My Little Brother

My little brother
He gets on my nerves
He used to smash the plates and cups
He even killed my birds

He always pesters Grandad
He's always up and down
He never looks after anything
Oh I wish he wasn't around

He's always in the living room
He's always up the stairs
He stops me doing my homework
Oh he makes me really scared

So that's my little brother
The little mischievous devil
Yes that's my little brother
Oh I wish I had another.

Kimberley Roache (10)
Wingate Junior School, Wingate

My Brother

My brother is so bossy
That's all he ever does
But when we get in a fight
He always gets a big fright
When we play on the PlayStation
He always gets beat
But when he gets beat
He always gets in a big huff with me.

Daniel Healer (10)
Wingate Junior School, Wingate

My Family

My little brother
He teases my mother
My sister is the same
She is a big fat pain

Then there's my mum
She has a big bum
My dad is quite mad
His pumps are really bad

My grandma makes nasty cakes
They really are as rough as rakes
My granda is very old
He hates it when it's cold.

Charlotte Patterson (10)
Wingate Junior School, Wingate

Fire

Fire is hot
Fire is fast
When it spreads
It will not last.

Tony Rowe (9)
Wingate Junior School, Wingate

Squeak Is The Best

Squeaking to each other
Squeak hasn't got a mother
Sweetcorn is the favourite treat
They love to eat
Holly is her sister
Pepsi too
Burrowing in the hay
Squeak sleeps to have her rest
Squeak is the best.

Hannah Blakelock (11)
Wingate Junior School, Wingate

Spring

S unshine in the sky
P eople playing out in the park
R ipe, sweet apples on the trees
I can see birds sing and fly
N ight - the moon comes out
G reen sweet grass growing.

McKenzie Mason (8)
Wingate Junior School, Wingate

Spring Is In The Air

Spring is in the air.
Children run around.
Birds make a tweeting sound.
In the spring the animals grow.
I hope that there is no more snow.

Kieran Baxter (9)
Wingate Junior School, Wingate

Lambs Are . . .

Lambs are fluffy
Lambs are soft
Lambs are happy
Lambs run around and play
Lambs are silly.

Demi Leigh Stanger (9)
Wingate Junior School, Wingate

Spring

S pring is in the air today
P retty flowers in the garden pots
R ed leaves growing on the trees
I n the field lambs eating grass
N ow new baby animals come out to play
G oodbye spring, it's time to say goodbye.

Dean Wallace (9)
Wingate Junior School, Wingate

The Game

The game was played today
Each team taking the ball
In a different way
Nearly all their team was tall

Our keeper Shay
Got hurt badly today
He got studded in the eye
He thought he was going to die

It was only in the last minute
When the greatest scorer Ray Winute
Stepped up to take a shot
And hit it off the keeper's bot.

0-0 was the score
There was nothing more
The gory game today
Was different in every way.

Jamie Robinson (10)
Wingate Junior School, Wingate

My Fab Friends

My friends are the very best,
Better than all the rest.
When I have a problem they come to me,
Until I'm really jumping for glee!

They are so great,
Especially my best mate.
She comes to my sleepovers and is never late,
Now that's a brill, brill mate.

Now you've learned about friends,
I hope this friendship never ends.
They are so cool like I've said,
Even better than my fab granda Ted!

Aimee Atkinson (10)
Wingate Junior School, Wingate

The Cats Next Door

Charley and Fizz are the best,
They are so better than the rest.
They climb up trees and jump around,
They catch lots of mice in just one pound.
Ginger and white,
Charley prowls during the night.
Black and white,
Fizz is the most stylish cat in sight.
They also purr when I stroke their fur,
Now they are two very cool cats!

Charlotte Lamb (10)
Wingate Junior School, Wingate

Monster

Some are ugly
Some are tall
Some are just scary
And some are small
Some you can see
And some are in my family.

Ryan Keating (11)
Wingate Junior School, Wingate

Swimming Around The Coral

Diving
down
deep
to the
hard brain
coral
and
seeing
urchins,
and sea anemones
sway
in the water.
Spot dazzling goldfish
hiding behind the colourful coral.
Watch
silver squid squirting ink
and
hermit crabs fighting.
See
plankton covering the entire sea.

Joshua O'Donnell (8)
Wingate Junior School, Wingate

The Coral Reef At The Bottom Of The Ocean

Diving
down
deep
into the
silent
turquoise-blue
ocean.
See the
colourful
coral reef -
rose,
purple,
lilac,
indigo,
maroon,
pink,
violet -
swaying in the
turquoise-blue
ocean.

Paige Elizabeth Ridley (9)
Wingate Junior School, Wingate

The Orange Starfish

The
orange
and
pink
starfish
sitting
on
the
rose,
scarlet,
indigo
rock
that is covered in lilac-mauve coral
in
the
turquoise-
blue
underworld
below
the
waves.

Adam Calvert (7)
Wingate Junior School, Wingate

The Sparkling Fish

As we
swim
around
the coral,
the giant,
grey sharks
are circling
us dangerously.
Darting around
nervously,
looking for
somewhere
to hide,
the big,
purple,
blue,
turquoise,
emerald
sea rushing
around us,
our sparkles
glimmer
in the light.

Jake Common (8)
Wingate Junior School, Wingate

Everybody Rap

Stop! Stop!
Save the world!
Save the world!
Pick up litter, help the environment
You are hurting the animals
You are hurting the animals

Don't drop litter
On the floor
If you see a bin
Use it more!

The animals don't like it
The animals don't like it
Stop now! Stop now!

Do you agree?
I said do you agree?
If you agree
Say 'yo' to me!

Joe Smith (7)
Wingate Junior School, Wingate

The World Of The Ocean

The
dazzling
rainbowfish
sparkled
through
the
golden
bright
coral
with
dangerous
great
white
sharks
circling
above
it.
The
wise
octopus
disappeared
into
the
indigo
ink.

Josh Craggs (8)
Wingate Junior School, Wingate

An Underwater World

Diving
down
into the
deep
blue
ocean.
Gliding,
shimmering,
dazzling
fish
swerve
in and out
of the
coral reef.
Enormous
sharks
circling
the
colourful
coral
silently
beady
eyes
searching.

Jake Blanchard (8)
Wingate Junior School, Wingate

Colourful Coral

Diving
below
the maroon
sea
is a
nice,
sparkly,
shiny
fish.
He lives
in a
colourful
coral reef.
Outside
of the
coral reef
are
spiky
sharks
swimming
in
circles.

Charlie Bruce (8)
Wingate Junior School, Wingate

The Amazing Ocean

Diving
down
into the
deep blue
aqua
water
of the
sea.
Sharks circling coral reefs.
Beautiful
sea anemones
walking
on the
purple rocks
of the
turquoise
ocean floor.
The sun's
dazzling
rays
brightening
the shallow
waters
with light.
Deep, deep down where pressure builds up, dark and glowing,
Fish still live.

Anthony Alan Teasdale (8)
Wingate Junior School, Wingate

Colourful Coral

Diving
down
below
into
the
deep
turquoise
water
we find
lavender,
violet,
pink,
lilac,
indigo,
purple
coral
with
fish
gliding
happily
and
shining
scales
glittering
in the
water.

Roy Stephenson (9)
Wingate Junior School, Wingate

Swishing Salty Sea

Under the swaying,
   salty sea live millions
      of busy fish landing and
         dashing - pink, purple, green, gold, red, yellow
                     and orange.
             The blueberryish sea
           shaded in purple sparkles.
         The spotty coral reefs at
        the bottom of the sea
       hides a queen fish
      named Strawberry with
       a red body and green
        spots that sparkle.
            A hungry shark tries to spot her.
           His hungry tummy rumbles
               as his teeth grind.

Sammy Jo Collins (8)
Wingate Junior School, Wingate

The Sea World

Diving down
into the
deep blue ocean
where
sharks
circle colourful
coral reefs
searching for food.
Unaware,
millions of
tiny, silvery, sparkling
fish dart
about playfully
in the lilac, blue and
indigo water.
A large purple
octopus with
eight swaying
tentacles is
sleeping in his
cold,
dark
cave.

Jordan John Hancock (8)
Wingate Junior School, Wingate

Reading Around The World

James' book is full of muck,
he smells it in the wind.
He reads it here, he reads it there,
he reads in his underwear.

It is written by Roald Dahl,
the book is called 'The Twits'.
He loves the pictures through the book,
he tries to trace them down.

He reads it at school,
he reads it in the pool,
but he's never got to read the ending,
so he feels like a fool.

Jack Fulton (10)
Wingate Junior School, Wingate

Wet Playtime

Find your friends
Go to the hall
Let's play Twister
Watch it, don't fall

Go for dinner
Have some meat
Come on
Let's eat

Now we've finished
let's find a seat
Oh no
We've been beat!

Now it's time
For us to draw
Time to play
A little bit more!

Jordan Hewett (8)
Wingate Junior School, Wingate

Wet Playtime

Go to the library
Let's read some books
Have some dinner
Speak to the cooks

Meet my friend
Let's play some games
Come on now agree
With me James

Let's do a jigsaw
It is a puzzle
Time to go
That was a muddle.

Jason Robson (8)
Wingate Junior School, Wingate

Two Friends

Jasmine Carter and Olivia Dunn
are friends today.
Using toys and injections full
we make animals better again.
Heads together, looking closely.
Who is the nurse?
Animals running everywhere.
Where have they gone?
I wish we could be friends forever.

Jasmine Carter (7)
Wingate Junior School, Wingate

Two Friends

Jordan Gray-Bostock and Jason Migue
are friends today.
Squirting shampoos and shower gels too,
make magical potions!
Heads together what will happen . . . ?
Will an alien pop up or will it go *bang?*
Standing there wondering
will we stay friends forever?

Jordan Gray-Bostock (9)
Wingate Junior School, Wingate

Everybody Rap

Can you help the environment?
Can you hep the environment?
Stop what you're doing
Stop what you're doing

Don't drop litter
Pick it up
Keep the environment clean
For all to be seen

Don't smoke
Because I don't want to choke
If you don't
I won't

Help the animals
Help their homes
Remember the rules
Do it now!

Do you agree?
I said do you agree?
If you agree
Say 'yo' to me!

Jack Roache (8)
Wingate Junior School, Wingate

Wet Playtime

Let's go to the library
Read some books
Why don't we play some games
Quick tidy up before the teacher looks

I wonder what we can play
Let's ask Mat
What will he say?
He says why don't we have a chat!

Come with me
Have some dinner
Enter a competition
You might become a winner!

Jordanna Simpson (9)
Wingate Junior School, Wingate

Two Friends

Abigayle Wilson and Grandma Harrison
Making stone, daisy and buttercup soup.
We stir until our arms ache
And then add grass and three leaf clovers.
I wish we could do this forever.
I wish we could be friends forever.

Abigayle Wilson (8)
Wingate Junior School, Wingate

Everybody Rap

Pick up the litter off the floor
See a bin, use it more.

Stop it now!
Stop it now!

Help the environment!
Help the environment!

What are you doing?
What are you doing?

Put up signs!
Put up signs!

Do you agree?
I said do you agree?
If you agree
Say 'yo' to me!

Remember the rules
Do it now!

Kaitlyn Rowe (8)
Wingate Junior School, Wingate

Everybody Rap

Can we save the environment?
Can we save the environment?
Don't drop litter!
Don't drop litter!
Can you save the world?
Can you save the world?
Do you like to help?
Do you like to help?

Don't drop litter on the floor
If you see a bin use it more

Put more signs up
Take your litter home
Because you don't drop
Litter on the floor

Do you agree?
I said do you agree?
If you agree
Say 'yo' to me.

Melissa O'Neill (9)
Wingate Junior School, Wingate

Young Writers Information

We hope you have enjoyed reading this book - and that you will continue to enjoy it in the coming years.

If you like reading and writing poetry drop us a line, or give us a call, and we'll send you a free information pack.

Alternatively if you would like to order further copies of this book or any of our other titles, then please give us a call or log onto our website at www.youngwriters.co.uk

Young Writers Information
Remus House
Coltsfoot Drive
Peterborough
PE2 9JX

(01733) 890066